Vocal / Piano

VOCAL POP
ORIGINAL KEYS FOR FEMALE SINGERS

T0056520

ISBN 978-1-4584-3792-1

HAL•LEONARD®
CORPORATION
7777 W. BLUEMOUND RD. P.O. BOX 13819 MILWAUKEE, WI 53213

Visit Hal Leonard Online at
www.halleonard.com

BAD ROMANCE

Words and Music by STEFANI GERMANOTTA
and NADIR KHAYAT

Moderately fast

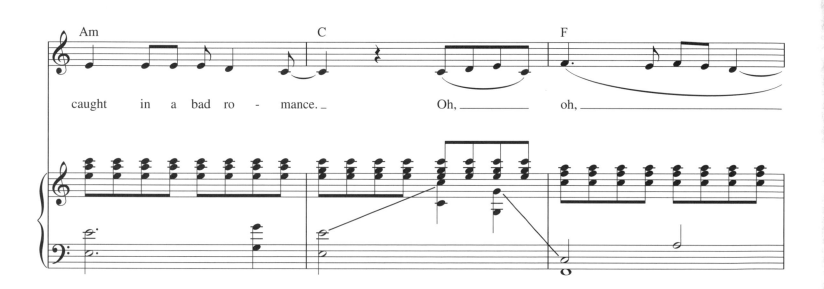

BEAUTIFUL

Words and Music by
LINDA PERRY

words can't bring us down, _____ oh, _____ no. _____ So don't you bring me down _____

_____ to - day. (Lead vocal ad lib.)

Don't you bring me down _____ to - day. _____ (Lead vocal ad lib.)

Don't you bring me down, _____ mm, _____ to - day. _____

BLACK HORSE AND THE CHERRY TREE

Words and Music by
KATIE TUNSTALL

black horse said, "Look this way," he said, "Hey la-dy, will you mar-ry me?" Whoo

hoo, whoo hoo. But I said,

"No, no, no, no, no, no." I said,

"No, no, you're not the one for me.

BLEEDING LOVE

Words and Music by JESSE McCARTNEY
and RYAN TEDDER

Moderately

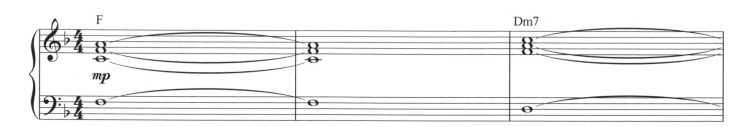

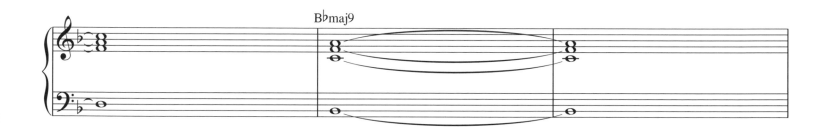

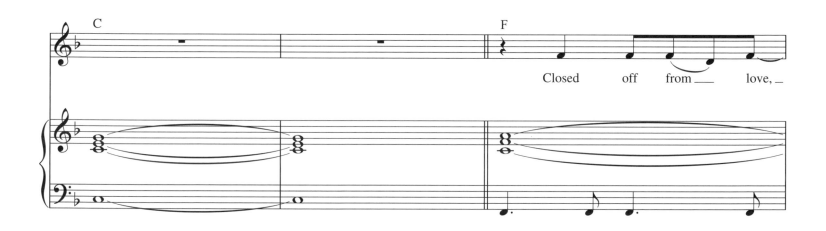

Closed off from ___ love, ___

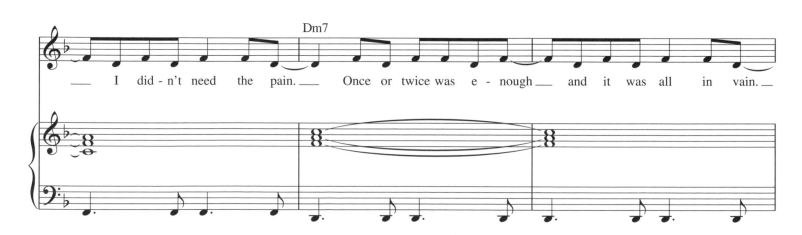

___ I did-n't need the pain. ___ Once or twice was e-nough ___ and it was all in vain. ___

To Coda

BREAKAWAY

from The Princess Diaries 2: Royal Engagement

Words and Music by BRIDGET BENENATE,
AVRIL LAVIGNE and MATTHEW GERRARD

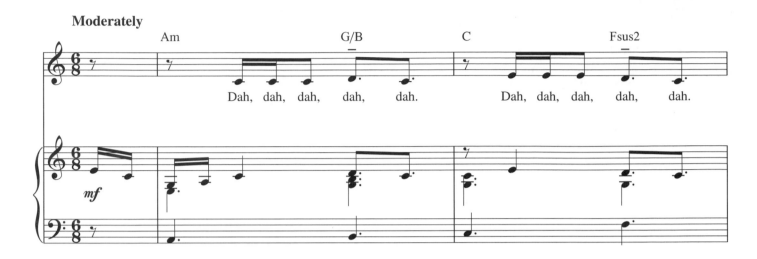

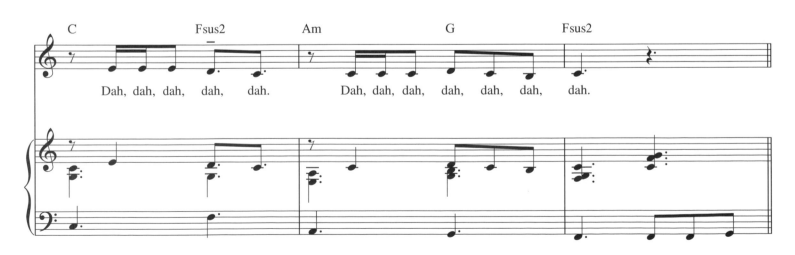

BREATHE

Words and Music by HOLLY LAMAR
and STEPHANIE BENTLEY

Moderately fast

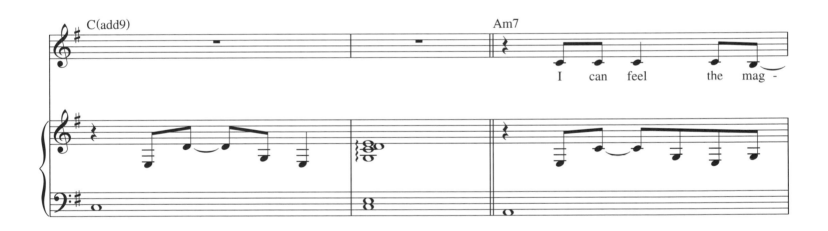

I can feel the mag-

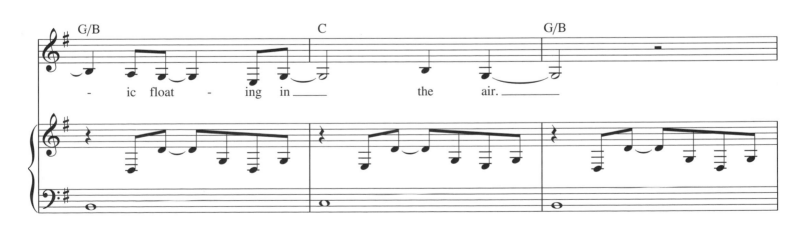

-ic float-ing in _____ the air. _____

Be - ing ____ with you ____ gets me that ____ way.

I watch the sun - light dance a - cross ____

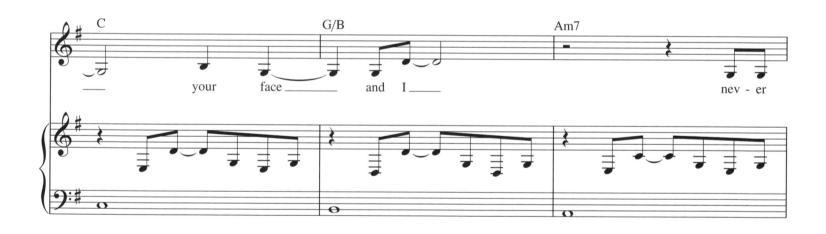

____ your face ____ and I ____ nev - er

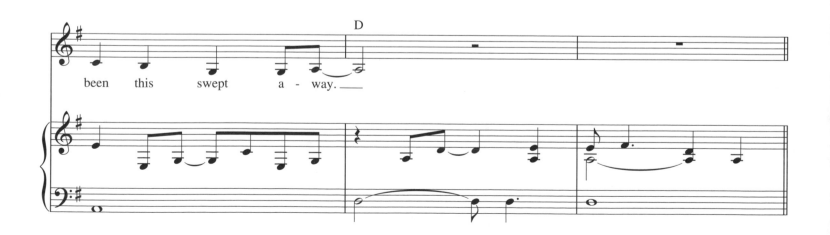

been this swept a - way. ____

BUILDING A MYSTERY

Words and Music by SARAH McLACHLAN
and PIERRE MARCHAND

Relaxed

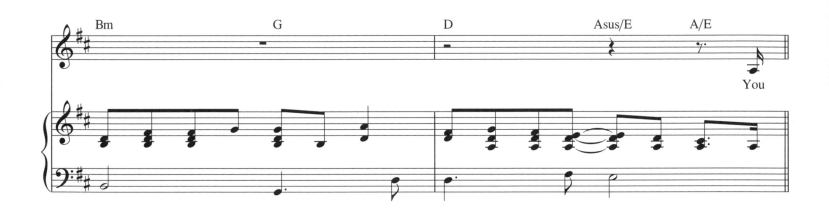

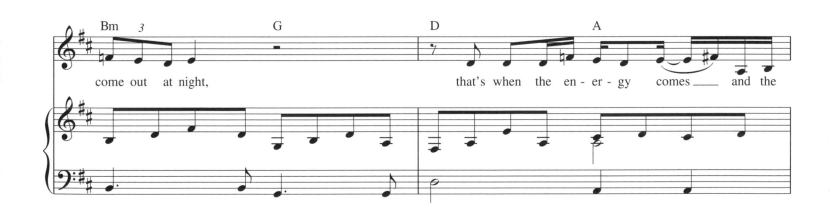

come out at night, that's when the en-er-gy comes ___ and the

dark side's _ light and the vam-pires roam. ___ You strut your ras-ta wear _ and your

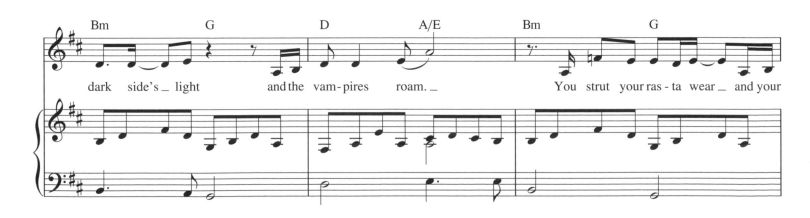

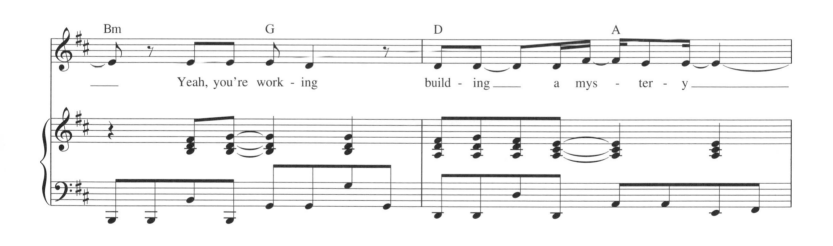

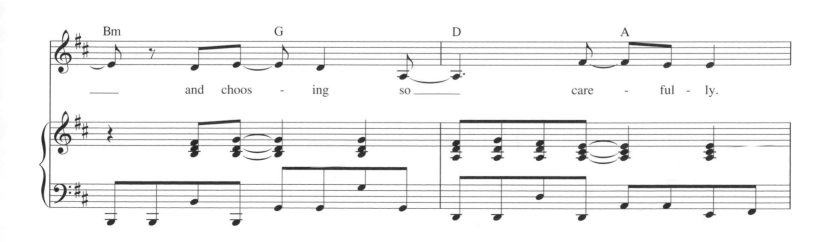

DON'T KNOW WHY

Words and Music by
JESSE HARRIS

Moderately slow

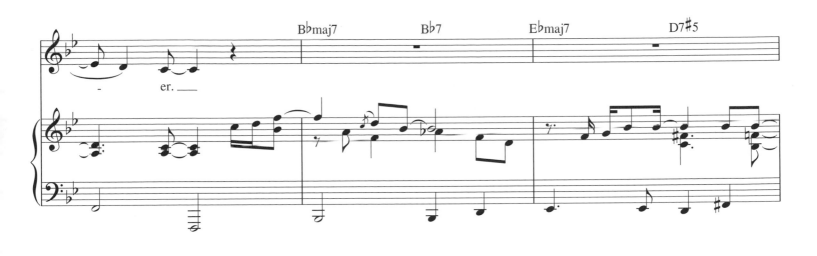

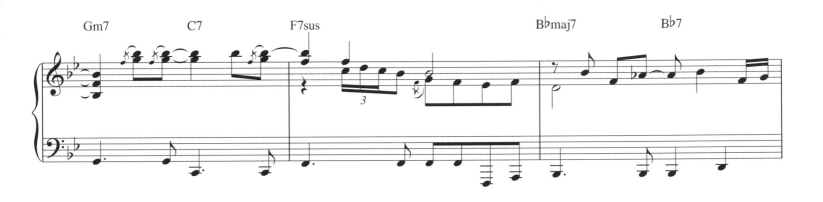

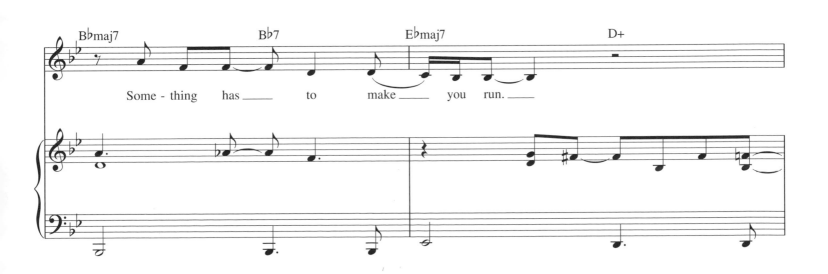

Some - thing has ____ to ____ make ____ you run. ____

HALO

Words and Music by BEYONCÉ KNOWLES,
RYAN TEDDER and EVAN BOGART

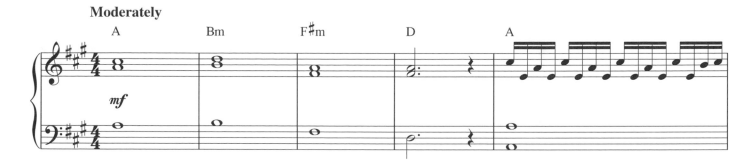

Remember those walls I built? Well baby, they're tumbling down, and they didn't even put up a fight; they didn't even make a sound.

* Vocals written an octave higher than sung.

*Vocals written at pitch

ha - lo, ha - lo.) Ha - lo. (I can see your) ha - lo, (ha - lo), ha - lo. (I can feel your)

ha - lo, (ha - lo), ha - lo. (I can see your) ha - lo, (ha - lo), ha - lo.

Hit me like a ray of sun burn-ing through my dark - est night.

You're the on - ly one that I want; 'think I'm ad-dict - ed to your light.

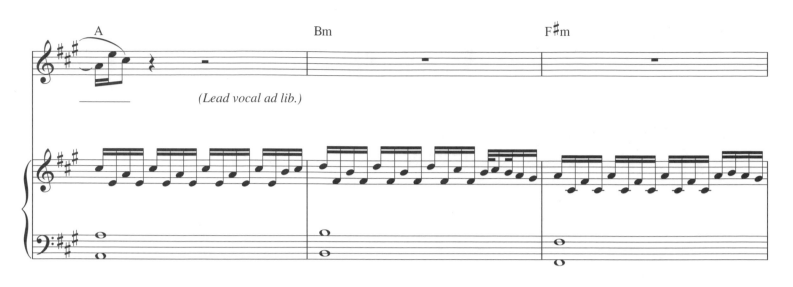

(Lead vocal ad lib.)

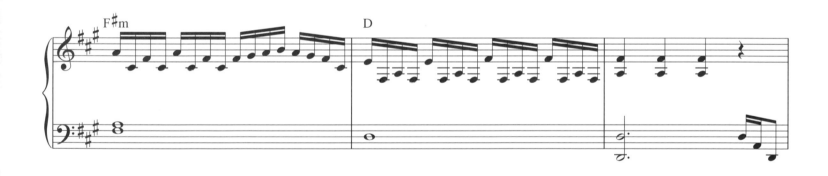

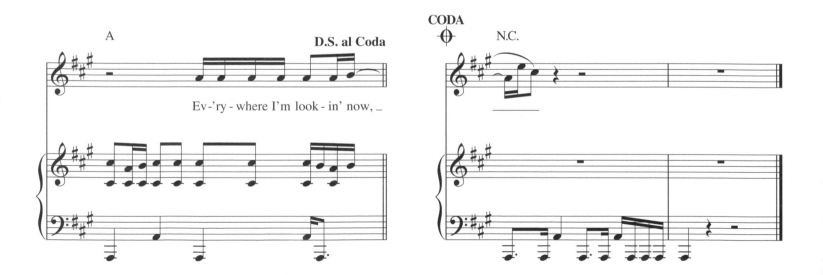

Ev-'ry - where I'm look - in' now, _

D.S. al Coda

CODA

N.C.

HERO

Words and Music by MARIAH CAREY
and WALTER AFANASIEFF

Slow Pop Ballad ($\quarternote$ = 60)

76

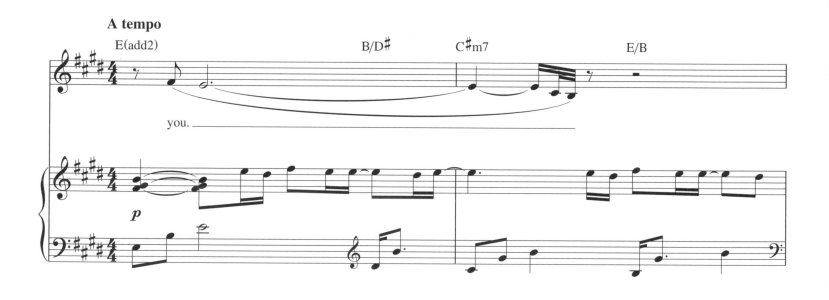

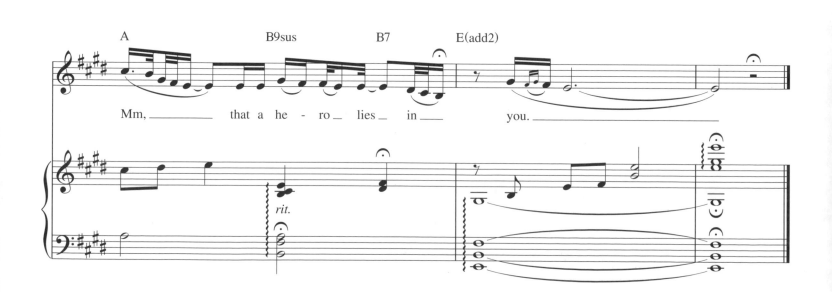

I DREAMED A DREAM
from LES MISÉRABLES

Music by CLAUDE-MICHEL SCHÖNBERG
Lyrics by ALAIN BOUBLIL,
JEAN-MARC NATEL and HERBERT KRETZMER

Moderately slow

I KISSED A GIRL

Words and Music by CATHY DENNIS,
MAX MARTIN, LUKASZ GOTTWALD
and KATY PERRY

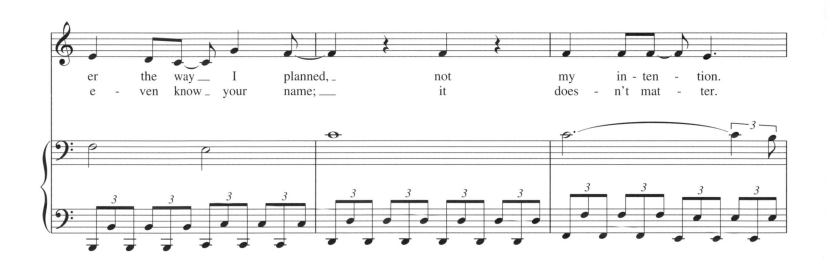

I WILL ALWAYS LOVE YOU

Words and Music by
DOLLY PARTON

Slowly, very freely

If __ I should __ stay, I would on - ly be in __ your

way, _____ so I'll __ go. __ But I __ know I'll __

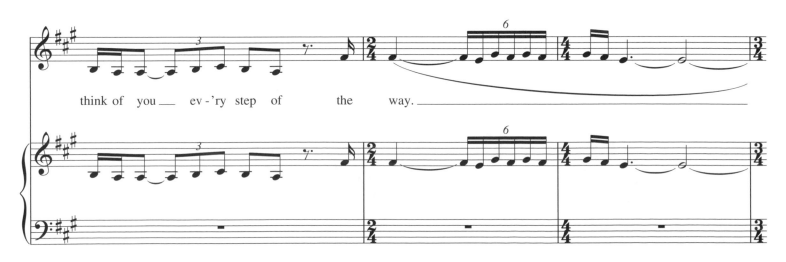

think of you __ ev-'ry step of the way. _____

Slowly, steadily

IF I AIN'T GOT YOU

Words and Music by
ALICIA KEYS

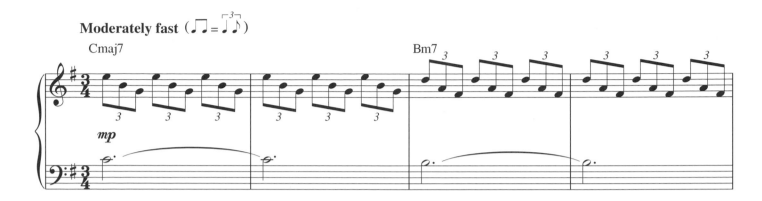

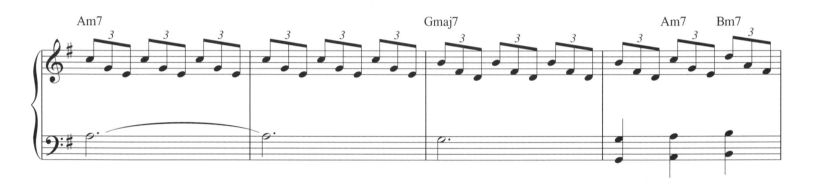

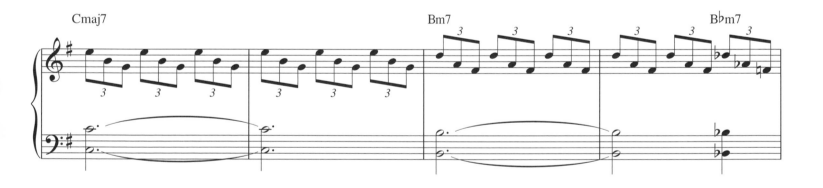

𝄋

Cmaj7

want it all, ___ but I don't want noth-in' at all ___ if it ain't ___

Bm7

Am7

you, __ ba - by, if I ain't got __ you, __ ba - by. Some peo-ple want

Gmaj7

Am7 **Bm7**

Cmaj7

dia-mond rings; _ some just want ev-er-y-thing, _ but ev-'ry-thing means

Bm7

B♭m7

Am7

Gmaj9

To Coda ⊕

noth-in' if I ain't got you, ____ yeah. ____ Some _ peo-ple

Am7 **Gmaj7**

I don't wnat noth-in' at all _____ if it ain't _ you, _ ba - by,

if I ain't got you, ba - by. _ Some peo-ple want dia-mond rings; _ some just want

ev - er - y - thing, _ but ev - 'ry - thing means noth - in' if I ain't got

you, _____ Yeah. _____

LOVE SONG

Words and Music by
SARA BAREILLES

walk the sev-en seas when I be-lieve that there's a rea-son to write ___ you a love ___

song to - day, ___ to - day, ___

yay, yay. ___

MY HEART WILL GO ON
(Love Theme From 'Titanic')
from the Paramount and Twentieth Century Fox Motion Picture TITANIC

Music by JAMES HORNER
Lyric by WILL JENNINGS

Moderately

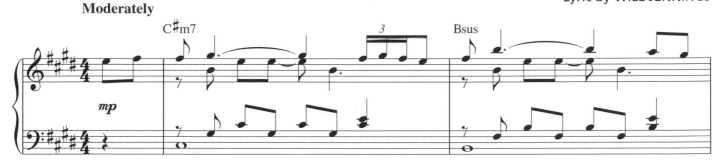

Pedal ad lib. throughout

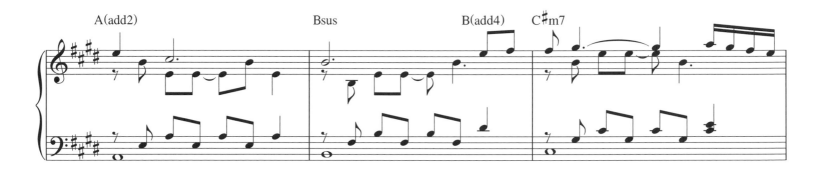

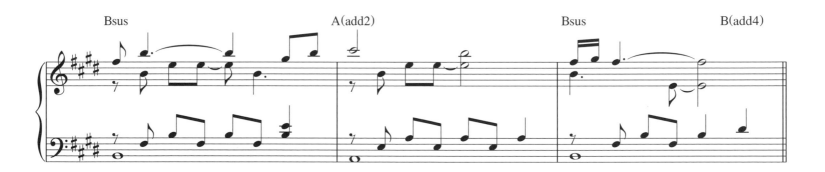

Ev - 'ry night in my dreams I see you, I

RAY OF LIGHT

Words and Music by WILLIAM ORBIT,
MADONNA, CLIVE MULDOON,
DAVE CURTIS and CHRISTINE LEACH

REHAB

Words and Music by
AMY WINEHOUSE

Moderately fast

They tried to make me go to re-hab, I ___ said ___

no, no, no. Yes ___ I've been black, but when ___

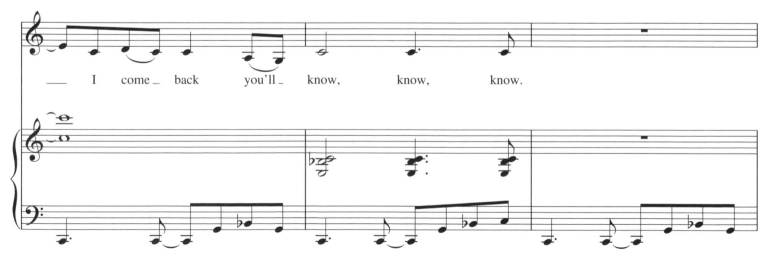

___ I come back you'll know, know, know.

on _____ the _____ mend. _____ And

it's not just my pride; _____

it's just 'til these

D.S. al Fine

tears _____ have _____ dried. _____ They

ROLLING IN THE DEEP

Words and Music by ADELE ADKINS
and PAUL EPWORTH

Moderately fast

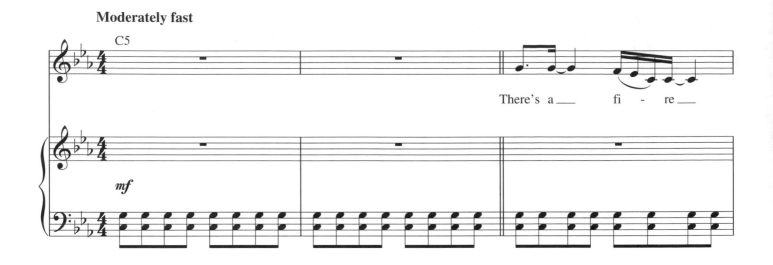

TEENAGE DREAM

Words and Music by LUKASZ GOTTWALD,
MAX MARTIN, BENJAMIN LEVIN,
BONNIE McKEE and KATY PERRY

Moderate Dance beat

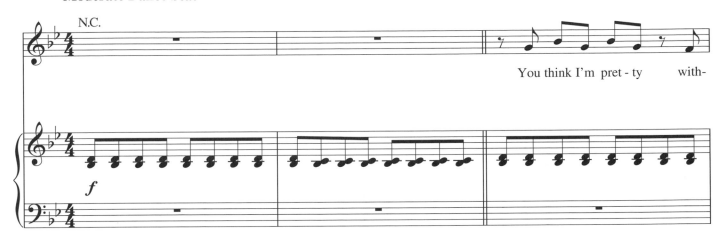

You think I'm pret- ty with-

out an- y make - up on. ___ You think I'm fun - ny when I tell the punch line wrong. ___

___ I know you get me, so I let my walls come down, ___ down. ___

WE FOUND LOVE

Words and Music by
CALVIN HARRIS

Moderately fast

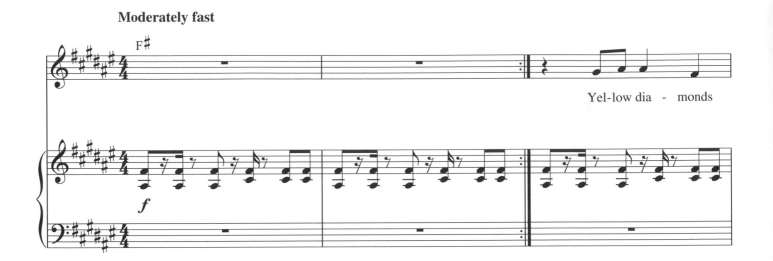

Yel-low dia - monds

in the light. ___ Now we're stand - ing side by ___ side.

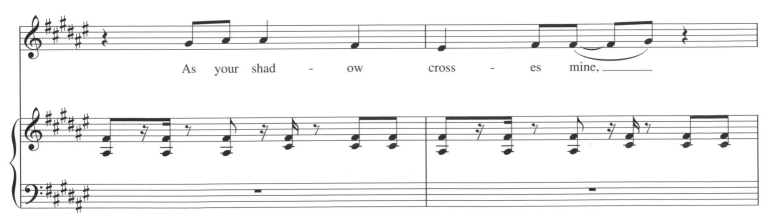

As your shad - ow cross - es mine, ___

We found love in a hope - less ___ place. We found love in a

hope - less place. ___ We found love in a hope - less ___ place. ___

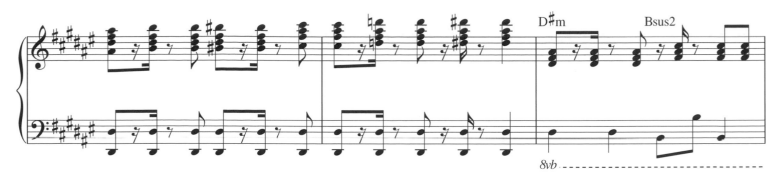

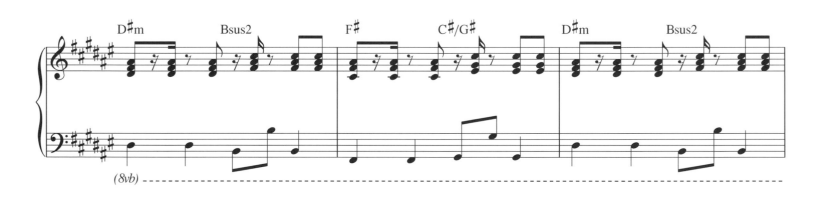

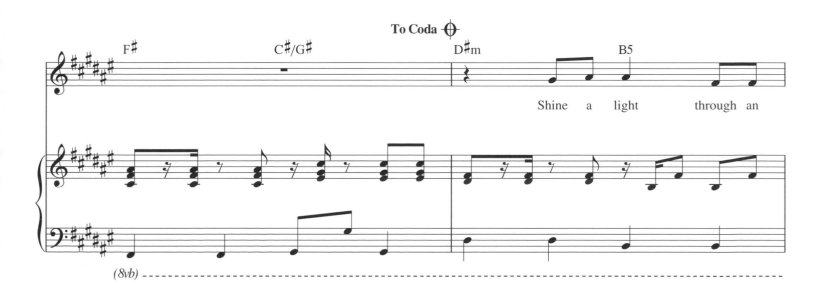

Shine a light through an

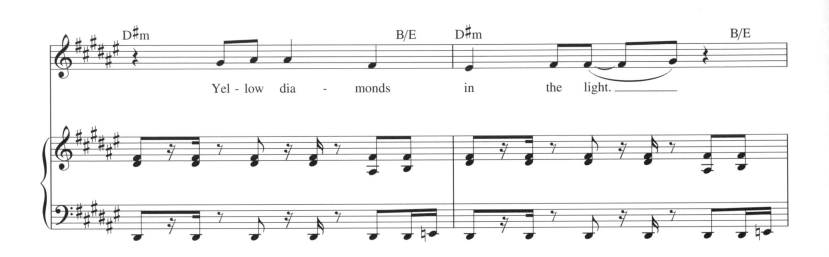

Yel - low dia - monds in the light.

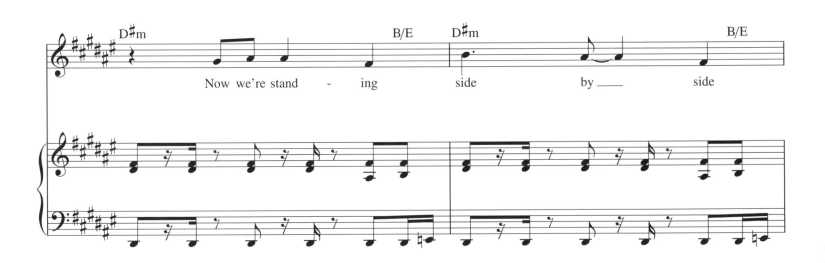

Now we're stand - ing side by side

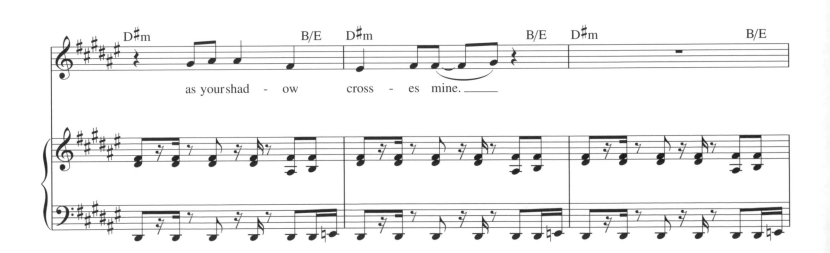

as your shad - ow cross - es mine.

YOU BELONG WITH ME

Words and Music by
TAYLOR SWIFT and LIZ ROSE

Moderately fast

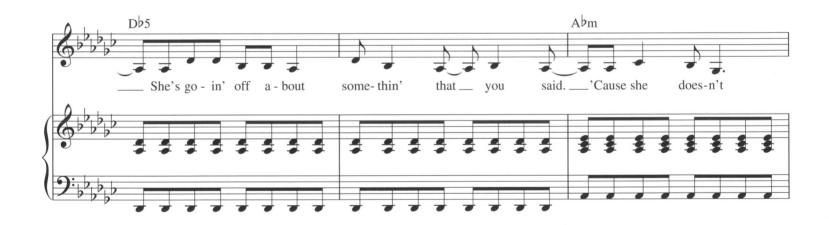

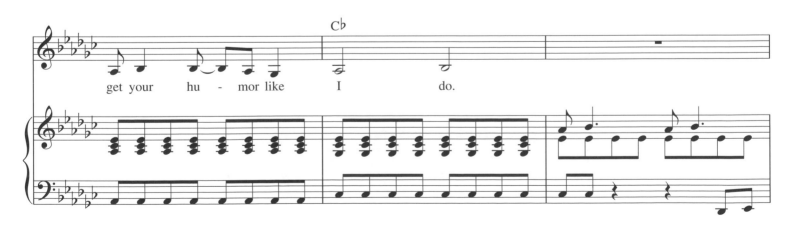

by, _____ you be - long _ with me? _____

You be - long _ with me. _____

Oh,   I   re-mem ber you